Bringing Church to the Elderly

Reaching the Forgotten Generation with a Message of Hope

Rev. James E. "Jimmy Mac" McNamara
and Lori McNamara

Christopher Matthews Publishing

www.christophermatthewspub.com

Boston, Massachusetts

Bringing Church to the Elderly

Copyright © 2016 by Lori McNamara

All rights reserved, except as permitted under the U.S. Copyright Act of 1976. No part of this publication may be reproduced, distributed or transmitted in any form or by any means, or stored in a database or retrieval system without the prior written permission of the author.

Editor: Jeremy Soldevilla
Cover design: Neil Noah
Images: Johnny Kenehan, Jamie Krause and
 Melonie Perry, Emaginative Imaging
 www.EmaginativeImaging.com

ISBN 9781938985874
ebook ISBN 9781938985881

Published by

CHRISTOPHER MATTHEWS PUBLISHING
www.christophermatthewspub.com
Boston

Printed in the United States of America

"This book defines the heart of a truly giving lady. Lori and her husband Jimmy found themselves called to offer a ministry inside an assisted living facility. They hadn't a clue as to how to proceed with these residents, but trusted their faith would provide a northstar.
    Indeed it did. Instead of just preaching scripture, they involved themselves in the residents' lives—becoming part of their extended family. They laughed and cried with them along the road and shared so many of their life milestones. And they were there to share an untimely milestone with Lori— she lost the love of her life, Jimmy, in 2014.
    In honor of Jimmy's amazing life, Lori has seen her mission to expand this exciting ministry. She and Jimmy have written this book to encourage others to tread this incredibly rewarding path to bring light and love to those most vulnerable, those most in need of spiritual illumination and friendship.
    A recent Facebook post shows Lori at the hospital sitting beside a resident, Russell. I can only imagine the comfort he finds in her presence. She's there . . . she's there.
    One of the residents once said of their service 'if I am dying, I *still* would be here.' And that's what this ministry is about—being there for the elderly.
    I think you'll find this book lively and fun, but perhaps most importantly, find it shows one *can* provide such a ministry. It *is* doable, and promises the ride of a lifetime."

— Johnny Kenehan, Emaginative Imaging

This book is dedicated to Jimmy–
my husband, my friend, my one true love.
You were my answered prayer—my gift from God—
And though our time together was short,
it was filled with love and life
beyond what I could have ever imagined.
You will always and forever be a part of me.

Now unto Him who is able to do exceeding abundantly above all that we ask or think . . .
                                —Ephesians 3:20

With special thanks:

... To my daughter, Jessica, and my son, Joshua, for loving me and supporting me and at times taking a back seat to those we had been called to minister to. There were times you stepped out of your own comfort zone to bless these precious souls and it made me so proud to watch you use the gifts and talents God gave you to bring joy to others. You will never truly know how much it meant to me having you by my side— those moments I will cherish forever. I love you both.

... To the special few that God called from the very beginning to support and sustain this ministry—Tyrone and Sharon Chew, Kurk and Lorilee Dorman, Daniel Nucum, Larry Fennell and John Wallace. You gave of yourselves unselfishly for more than just a season. This ministry would not be what it is today if not for the love and commitment you showed to every resident and to Jimmy and me as well. You will always have a very special place in my heart.

... To my church family at Valley Bible Fellowship Las Vegas and beyond. The number is far too great to even begin to list each and every one of you by name that has helped bring smiles to the faces of our elderly family. Young and old alike came and served and made a difference in the lives of these special people. You answered the call to "look after widows in their distress." Your deeds have not gone unnoticed. Your reward will be great.

... To Pastor Jim Crews for your listening ear, for your encouragement, for your prayers, and most of all for not giving up on me and the mission I felt God had placed on my heart to expand this ministry—a ministry that Jimmy and I had grown to love. Your support has given me the courage and strength to move forward and to trust God in this new season of my life. Thank you for believing in me.

... To Pastor Doug Loman for being an amazing friend and spiritual mentor to my husband. You saw in him the potential and gifting to do that which even he didn't realize he could do— preach. You, alone, have been with us since the very beginning of this ministry—you stood with us as we navigated through the unknown—prayed for us through the heartache and loss— and supported us with every opportunity you had, including ministering the word of God. Thank you for continuing to be a part of what God is doing even now.

. . . To the residents and staff of Heritage Springs Senior Center for letting us be a part of your lives. You loved on us and included us in your many special occasions – in holidays and birthdays— in weddings and memorials. We laughed together and we cried together. We became family. Your willingness to let us come into your home and share our faith and our lives blessed us beyond words and changed us forever. We will never be the same.

. . . Finally, to my husband and best friend, Jimmy— God brought you into my life to be more than just a husband and friend – you were my strength, my joy, my hope, and my love. You were my inspiration. You believed in me and helped me believe in myself. You pushed me beyond my limits and encouraged me to be the woman God called me to be. You taught me much about love and life and serving others. Because of you this ministry began and because of you this ministry will continue. Thank you for an amazing legacy.

Table of Contents

Foreword i
Introduction 1
Chapter 1: Why Bring Church to the Elderly? 5
    Mickey 9
Chapter 2: Where do We Start? 13
    Lowell 18
Chapter 3: Who Is Going To Show Up? 21
    Joe 30
Chapter 4: What Does It Look Like? 35
    Sheriff Joe 39
Chapter 5: Topics for Sermons 41
    Cleaveland 54
Chapter 6: Funding 57
    Gracie 61
Chapter 7: Final Thoughts 63
Jimmy's Story 67
About the Authors 69
320 Ministries International 71

Foreword

Life has a way of taking twists and turns that none of us expect. We plan, we prepare, we dream—and then in a moment... all is changed forever. As I write this, I am preparing my usual egg and toast for breakfast. My husband, Jimmy, made me this breakfast every morning before I went to work. Never did I expect that one morning it would end so abruptly.

Jimmy finished writing this book less than six months before the Lord took him home on November 20, 2014. It was our dream and passion to expand the work of ministering to the elderly in a greater capacity—that of providing resources and tools that would enable others with that same heart and passion to begin their own ministry to the elderly. This book was one of those tools.

Jimmy had a sense in his final months that God was telling him to prepare for a change, to tie up loose ends, and to take care of immediate business and personal plans which included writing this book. At the time, we both thought it was for a prepared move out of state—a change of location that would enable us to further God's call on our life. Neither one of us thought the Lord was actually preparing to call Jimmy home.

I sense an urgency now, more than ever, to get the Word out without delay to those that are unable to seek it for themselves. This book gives simple instructions for doing just that. It was written to instruct others on how to bring church to the elderly; specifically those that are unable to physically attend a service outside of their assisted living residence or nursing home.

We want to give those that are at the edge of eternity an opportunity to hear the Word of God. To share with them that salvation is by grace alone through faith in Jesus Christ and to know God's perfect plan for their life after death—eternity in heaven. This was our hearts' desire and a dream that began with my husband and me over six years ago.

I pray this book will spark a flame of passion and desire in individuals and churches alike to begin reaching out to this sometimes forgotten generation.

God has said in His Word, "religion that God our Father accepts as pure and faultless is this: to look after orphans and widows in their distress." (James 1:27 NIV). That is our heart and we pray it is your heart as well.

—Lori McNamara

Introduction

In 2008, my husband and I were asked by our church to lead a service at an assisted living center. Neither one of us had any experience in such an endeavor. We showed up the first Sunday in faith and trust that God would lead us every step of the way—and He did. It has now been seven years, and the church, with members ranging in ages from 70 to 101, still meets faithfully every Sunday.

This book will provide insight and direction on how to "bring church" to a senior living center in your own community. We will walk you through the stages of choosing a location, recruiting volunteers, selecting a service format, and deciding on the necessary equipment and supplies that you will need. We will share some of the special needs of the elderly and how to best provide for those needs. Sermon topics and music selections are also a very critical part of the service. We will expound on those along with the importance of knowing your audience.

What we have shared in this book is what has worked for us and for our congregation. We understand that all churches have their own unique style of conducting a church service, and you may have other ideas that work best for you. There are no set rules on what works and what doesn't. God will lead you. Our goal in writing this book was to provide a starting point for those that have never taken on a ministry such as this or are seeking new ideas to enhance their current program.

We have so many beautiful and unforgettable memories from our years of serving the elderly in this capacity. Dispersed throughout the book you will read some individual stories of the precious souls we met and were blessed to have known. We have shared many joyful and heartwarming moments with them and their families.

As you embark on this wonderful adventure—sharing life and love with these unique individuals—we are certain you will experience the same joy and fulfillment that we have experienced. You will find this to be one of the most rewarding times of your life, and you will truly and firmly believe in the words: "It is more blessed to give than to receive." (Acts 20:35 KJV)

My husband Jimmy has now since gone home to be with the Lord, but what he left behind and the message he shared I pray will continue on for generations to come. I invite you all to be a part of it!

—Lori McNamara

Chapter 1: Why Bring Church to the Elderly?

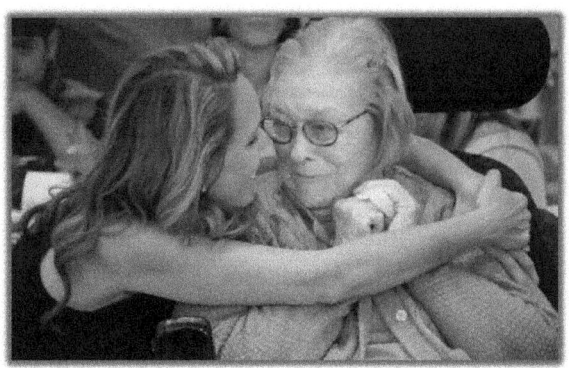

Is there really a need?

"Why is there a need for bringing church to the elderly?"

I've found this to be an awkward question at times, but also a very valid one.

A rational person would consider that anyone up in their years would have already been set in their beliefs and how they would spend eternity. We have found that not to be the case. As a matter of fact, many of the people who have been a part of our lives over the past several years have been uncertain in their thoughts and beliefs.

I recall a woman I'll refer to as Mary. Mary was raised a Catholic in the South. Having attended parochial school all her life (just as myself), she was afraid of God. She had been taught that He was a God of vengeance more so than love. She feared His wrath and when hearing and reading more about the love of Jesus Christ, she began to question what she had been taught all her life.

Reading the Bible was not something she had been taught, and although the truth had been sitting before her all her life . . . she was never encouraged to read it.

Being able to read His Word and read the stories herself about all that Jesus did while He was on earth, and how "God so loved the world that He gave His only begotten Son"(John 3:16 KJV), she began to have a relationship with God rather than belong to a religion.

The folks who attend the services are there for many reasons. Some are there because they want to continue worshipping in a community based group—what they can recall as a church. Others are there out of an obligation to "attend church on Sunday."

Still others attend out of a need for some kind of comfort and assurance that "everything is going to be alright." And believe it or not, we've got some folks who show up just out of curiosity.

In our ministry, the room where we hold our services is open to the main corridor of the facility, and it's difficult to walk past the room and not see what's going on.

I've been blessed to have a wife who has an incredible voice and God-given talent to sing, and that alone attracts many to the services.

We have been thanked over and over again by the residents of the Assisted Living Home for bringing church to them every Sunday. Had it not been for these services the majority of them would not be able to attend church. At least 90% of our congregation are either on walkers, in wheelchairs, or motorized scooters. There is no way they would be able to leave on a regular basis to attend a church service outside of the building.

These beautiful people's ages range from the early 70's to the early 100's. We even have one gentleman who is 98 years old and has moved away to a more constant care facility, yet his daughter brings him back twice a month for service because there is none where he now resides.

We have non-residents who have heard of our services and come to join in and worship with us because they love being around the residents and love spending time with them and hearing their stories. They also enjoy the older hymns and songs that we play (which we'll cover more in a later chapter).

So the need is there—and because of the need, we are there.

Mickey

y name is Mickey ~ like the mouse." This is how she introduced herself to us. She was in her mid- to late 70's, outspoken, and knew what she had to have in her life and if it worked out for others; well, that was just fine.

Mickey rallied the troops, all four of them plus herself, and approached the staff at the assisted living center for a Christian church service. Our church answered the call, as did my wife and I. I'll never forget the first time I preached a sermon there.

Actually it was the first time I had preached a sermon *anywhere*. I was nervous; the sweat rings on my shirt proved that. There were sixteen people sitting before me. They were waiting on hearing "The Word." What I saw before me was a jury of twelve and four alternates.

I made my way through that first day determined to do better the next. As I completed my sermon and closed with a prayer, I knew I would have to say something to each person before they left.

Mickey was the first to make her way to me. Nothing stood between her and myself; there was no podium, no chairs; just what appeared to be a runway, and all the traffic was headed in my direction.

She extended her hand to me prepared to shake mine. As she did, she covered both our hands with her left, and as her arthritic hands touched, her furrowed eyebrows relaxed as she said "Don't worry, your second time will be better."

Not what I was expecting to hear, but I suppose it was better than could have been expected.

As the weeks became months, our little ministry had outgrown the craft room where we had met since my first day of preaching. Soon, we were moved into the two gathering rooms downstairs.

One was an ice cream bar, complete with big screen television, a bar with three stools, tables and chairs. The tables were moved outside to the patio, and I realized quickly that I would need a podium from which to preach, so I built one.

I also built a wooden tray which would hold the juice cups and bread and a collection plate since these wonderful folks wanted to donate to the ministry.

The first Sunday they were all put into use.

Mickey came to me and said "This church is lacking something, and I'll take care of it for next Sunday."

She wouldn't elaborate, and I had learned not to question Mickey or her motives. She was a confident woman who knew right from wrong, so I gave her all the leeway she required.

The next Sunday, Mickey reached into the bag on her walker and produced a cross. It stood about 14 inches tall, and she simply stated as she handed it to me "This needs to be seen at each and every service."

I simply stated "Yes, ma'am."

It's one of the legacies Mickey left behind. Mickey insisted on everyone being punctual for church, and she always dressed the part as well.

There were a couple of days when Mickey was not in church. At each of those times, I was given a message that Mickey wasn't having a good day and wanted us to know she wouldn't be in the service.

We asked to visit with her, but she denied each and every request. Mickey suffered from Parkinson's disease, and she would have occasions when the tremors were too much for her to control. There was a "lady" present who wished not to be embarrassed. I honored that request.

Mickey attended practically every service we had in that building up until she went home to be with the Lord. She left us suddenly.

Mickey was at church the Sunday before she passed away. She seemed fine; nothing was out of the ordinary. It was a shock for me. This was one of the "Original Five," as they've come to be known to us. She was eloquent, elegant and one of God's kids.

I was asked to perform her memorial service and I stood before each person with tears in my eyes as I described this wonderful woman.

To this day, that same cross that Mickey brought to our little church is displayed at every service. Mickey was seventy-seven years old when she died.

Chapter 2: Where do We Start?

This question is answered probably more easily than you think.

We were fortunate. We actually had a facility call and ask our church if there was a possibility that someone could come over and hold a service at their location. It was convenient; less than one city block away.

Ironically, I was asked by my pastor after just two services to take over this ministry and I had never preached a day in my life!

Once we became established doing these services, requests from other places began to come in. Sadly enough, no one had been schooled in how to do a remote service such as this, so our pioneering days began.

I can tell you that when you finish reading this book and you feel God is calling you to add this to your church outreach, a simple phone call to practically any assisted living center or nursing home in your area will be welcomed.

Most of the activity directors deal with time slots to fill. In our case, five of the residents approached the activity director as well as the staff and requested they find a church to come and "bring church" to them. As a side note, I personally performed the memorial services of each one of these five beautiful people as they have each gone home to be with the Lord.

At our location, there are two services provided: one for the Catholic faith and ours which is considered

Christian/Protestant. We have had many Catholics, Jews and Mormons attend our services as well.

Your place or mine?

One of the key elements to this ministry is where it will be conducted. We have found it is best at the place of the residency. The residents feel they are best being served by having the convenience of staying on property, and the liability issues are greatly reduced versus transporting to your church.

People are more apt to come to the service if it is close by, and the underlying "need" to dress up is greatly reduced.

Please keep in mind that it is greatly encouraged to have as many people from your church visit the facility from time to time. "Nothin' says lovin' . . ." than to see folks show up just to say "Hi."

Location-Location-Location

Oftentimes, the location, or room that your service will be held in, is not a choice but one option that the facility offers to your ministry. When we first began our ministry, we were in a 10 x 12 room where half of it was being used as a storeroom for chairs. After our third week, the attendance had grown from the original five people to sixteen. We were moved upstairs to the craft room where tables and chairs were afforded us.

After a mere two months, we outgrew that room and are currently in the main room with an adjoining visiting area. We have anywhere from 20 to 45 people in attendance.

The best location in the building for a church service is one that is easily accessible and has plenty of room for chairs, walkers and motorized scooters. Our room opens to another via a large double door entry, so if someone doesn't want to be in the main room, they can sit in the "back of the church," remain secluded, but still be a part of the service.

Oftentimes new residents who are uncertain of what is going on around them or don't care to be an active part of the service can be found there. We always make it a point to go to them at the end of the service, shake their hands and let them know we were glad they were there . . . always make everyone feel welcomed.

We've had some special occasions that allowed us to bring our services outside to the patio area. With the doors open and with the cooling of temperatures in the Las Vegas desert in springtime, we were able to bring in some special guests and singers that drew a crowd of almost one hundred people.

We try to keep everything as new and fresh as possible. Stay true to the Word, but present it in such a way as to keep everyone's attention.

Lowell

owell.
What a hard card to read. I'd never seen him stand, but I'm certain he's probably at least six foot six inches tall. His long jaw and slender frame follows a long line to his long legs.

He refused to use a regular wheelchair. He got around in a rolling chair and was always moving about in reverse using those long legs as his horsepower. Having run into a few walls and an occasional chair or table (not to mention a few other residents), he was asked to "reverse the reverse" and drive facing his destination. Still not using his hands to move himself; he spidered his way around using his feet to "pull" himself.

What makes this man so special is his life's story. Lowell was a television western cowboy. His twenty year span of "ridin' tall in the saddle" brought him enjoyment and pleasure. He's a bit shy when it comes to telling of his career, but once he gets started he's a hard book to close.

His hands are long and now suffer the signs of arthritis. But Lowell doesn't hesitate to use them to help tell his stories. Once you sit down, he knows you're serious about listening, and the gleam in his eyes sparkles like a Tiffany diamond. His voice is deep but soft; almost a whisper that I think he uses to get people to sit closer to him. It's a trait that I've thought about using a time or two myself.

When he gets through with telling one of his stories, he's ready to leave. If you're insistent, he'll grab another one out of his Stetson, but usually two is his limit.

He loves to hear stories of how others enjoy the old black and white westerns and how they're still alive in people's hearts today. I believe that's some of the charm of this gracious man. He likes knowing that he's touched someone's heart and life.

I believe we all like that.

Chapter 3: Who is Going to Show Up?

Residents

There is no set answer to this question. The residents will come out of commitment or need or if they have nothing else to do. There's no other way to put it, but you'll find this to be a fairly true statement.

One of the things we do prior to each service is what we lovingly refer to as the "Pre-game warm-up!" Our service begins at 9:15 a.m. Our starting time is critical because it allows the residents to finish their breakfast, go back to their rooms to freshen up, and come back down for church.

At 9:00 a.m., my wife is sitting on her stool with guitar in hand and at her microphone singing and playing some songs. For those who are not yet in their seats, they come in and feel like they "arrived just on time." Anyone who is there for the first time can simply hear the music and come in to listen.

We offer "valet parking" for all the walkers. When someone comes in, we have a volunteer welcome them, help them get seated and take the walker out to the hallway or the adjacent room. This allows for less clutter and ease of others making their way into the room. I use it to my advantage as well. If they don't have their walkers with them, they can't leave! I've oftentimes made that announcement and brought tons of laughter along with it. Remember that these people love to laugh and have a need to laugh!

If 9 a.m. rolls around and my wife is not singing and playing, then I grab my guitar and only the Lord knows what's going to come out of my mouth. It could be "You Are My Sunshine" or "Stand by Me." One Sunday I had a room full of people between the ages of 75 and 93 singing "You don't have to call me darlin' . . . darlin' . . . ," an old David Allen Coe song.

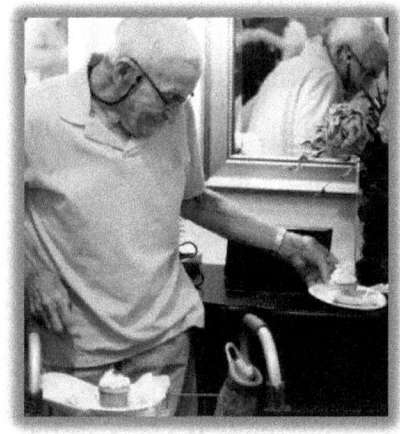

I believe in "keeping it real," and these songs are a part of many of their pasts. I took the time to download the words to many of the songs that were popular during the 30's, 40's and 50's, and it brings back some amazing smiles.

Your mileage may vary—but believe me when I tell you that your congregation is also your audience. Keep their attention and they'll be like little sponges waiting for the Word of God to enter into their hearts! We actually have some residents who arrive 45 minutes early for the service.

Volunteers

Volunteers are a key to any ministries' success, and you can never have too many of them. Over the past six years there have been dozens who have either assisted at one or two services or throughout the entire history of the ministry.

They have built relationships with many of the residents and love them as they do their own families. It is important—actually vital—that these people are recognized from time to time in front of the congregation. They give selflessly and lovingly, and even though I embarrass them when I do it, it's always good to know that you are appreciated.

Cherish these people—they are your ministerial spine. They support you and your ministry.

Always continue to seek more help. It's been a rule of thumb that 5% of the church volunteers perform the work for the remaining 95%. It's easy to wear out your volunteers. We have a sound system that we set up each Sunday morning. Our volunteers usually help unload it and set it up. Once every few weeks or so, my wife and I will arrive early and do all this by ourselves. It gives our volunteers a break and allows them to visit more with the residents as they come into the room. It's just a way of showing a little appreciation without taking away the importance of the work they do for the ministry.

One other way is to discuss gift cards for your volunteers with your lead pastor or whoever is in charge of allocating funds within your main church. It is greatly appreciated by those who receive them, and quite honestly, this reward system makes them want to do more.

Our ministry was honored with "Volunteer of the Year" award and was presented with a plaque by our assisted living facility. It hangs proudly in the entry to our church office. When people see and hear things about your ministry, the easier it is to get help when you need it.

There are many times when other ministries in our church will connect with our elderly ministry. The Youth Group, oftentimes bringing cookies, will stop by and visit just to listen to the stories of those who have been a part of forming the history of our great nation. We have elderly residents who attend our services that were some of the first employees of IBM; one was a figure skater with some of the world's greatest names in the sport; one played on the original American

Negro Baseball League; and one was a famous TV and western movie cowboy. You get to learn so much by sitting down and listening. Others come by just to sit with the residents and watch television or a movie with them.

I have been fortunate in my life to have some friends who will come over and bring some amazing talents with them. There is a gospel trio who has raised the roof off the place; a Christian singer/songwriter who has received numerous Dove awards and Grammy nominations who flew in from Nashville and helped celebrate the 5th year anniversary of our ministry; a presidential impersonator who we had to convince some people that he was NOT George Bush; and so many others over the years.

Be sure that if you're going to involve others that they are aware of any house rules and regulations that exist within the facility. A Schedule of Events is easily obtained from the Activity Director who is usually always happy to share it with you so there is no conflict with the residents on their daily activities.

Any children should be carefully supervised and reminded that these people can (and are) usually fragile and cannot be moved around or "handled."

If someone needs assistance with sitting or standing, always call upon the staff to make these accommodations. Specially trained personnel know the proper techniques to support an elderly person when they are going to sit or stand. Pulling on someone's arm could cause serious injury.

The main thing is to enjoy their company and allow them to enjoy yours.

Children

It's amazing what the "little things" in life are to some people. In this case, it happens to be the "little people," and yes—I'm talking children. We've had many, let me rephrase that—LOTS of kids visit during our time during the ministry.

Kids are a staple in our lives. They're fresh, playful, obstinate, loving, loud, soft, shy and obnoxious. They can bring you to tears and bring you to laughter at the drop of a hat. You never know what will come out of their mouths, and trust me when I say, anything is fair pickings from their honesty.

"You're REALLY OLD" has been heard a few times, and it brought laughter to the elderly and looks of shock on the parents' faces.

There are some who will walk up to a resident and just put their finger on their hands to "see what wrinkles feel like."

They are blatantly honest. There are a few of the residents who see the kids and are immediately drawn to them. We have one lady who reaches into her purse and pulls out a dollar for each child. When she runs out of cash, she asks the parents to remain there while she returns to her apartment for more.

Others carry lollipops and even some do crafts and carry them with them as prizes for the surprised little ones. It's amazing how this magnetism is drawn between the vast difference in ages and generations.

I've been told that many of these people have family living in other cities and aren't able to see their own children, grandchildren, and oftentimes great-grandchildren. Sadly enough, many live in town and just don't take the time to visit. We encourage and invite as many couples with small children to visit with us. I once saw a woman who was ninety-eight-years old sit through an entire service holding the hand of a ten-year-old little girl who was visiting with her parents. I've never seen this lady more at peace than on that day.

The things that we take for granted on a daily basis, are like a golden Christmas present to others. No wonder Jesus said "Suffer the little children to come unto me."(Luke 18:16 ASV) He knew their value to others.

Joe

is name was Joe.
He was an Italian and Catholic. His five foot five inch stature seemed diminutive since he was always seated. He had a personality that was either brash or as cute as a 5-year-old kid; both of which shared about 50% of his life equally.

Joe was crafty; always looking for a way to either become your best friend or how he could make you think he was your best friend. He had a cunning way about him, and although I never knew what he had done to make a living most of his life, I can't help but think some sort of sales had to have been involved. He was a master at words.

His accent hailed from either the Bronx or Brooklyn. It seemed to shift from one to the other depending on the conversation. There were times when he was "the boss"—tough and confident, yet at the same time, trying to convince others to agree with him as he attempted to believe in himself.

There were times when he was the center of the room. And then there were the times when he was completely vulnerable—not begging for attention, but was hurting physically and seemed to need someone more than anyone was willing to give only because they'd seen him cry "wolf" more times than once.

Joe wandered past our church service several times and appeared intrigued, when he noticed the live music being performed. He saw something that was more powerful than the messages being shared. Joe saw a microphone. From that moment forward, he knew he wanted to go to church. He would study our services; making mental notes of when the music would be performed. He became a regular, and as a part of our services, we would ask some of the congregation to sing along with us and would hand them a microphone so they could take more of a part. That's all it took for Joe—he knew he would have to attend and wait for his chance to hold the microphone.

We all thought Joe was a frustrated lounge act that never made it past an Italian restaurant's bar in New York. His signature line was priceless; he would repeat the last word of the song three times. It never failed—it was the same every time.

He took his turn one Sunday at the end of the service stating that he just felt like he had to share a beautiful song that was laid on his heart. His sincerity was overwhelming, and the people at the service were in total astonishment as this "miracle" appeared from within a guy who came across as a gutsy Italian with "possible connections" and a quick fuggetaboutit response.

He sang his song, and was given a round of courtesy applause. It was all very condescending to me, but he appreciated it.

I thanked him and reminded him that since this is a church service, we'd like to keep the music along the theme of Christian songs or hymns.

He said, "No problem," and went on his way.

I had noticed a few of the members rolling their eyes as he left so I wanted to pursue the issue a bit further. I mentioned the situation to the activities director who came across with a hearty laugh and let me know that when it's karaoke night, it's all they can do to get the microphone away from him! He feels like he should sing every song, and if not, well then he just should!

I smiled as I learned just a little bit more about my friend. Regardless of his singing abilities, he was coming to church and that was the most important part to me.

Joe's health began to deteriorate. I stopped by one day during the week and made it a point to go see him. He was sitting alone in the game room upstairs pulling the handle on the slot machine. It was something he enjoyed doing. It cost nothing to play, and you couldn't win the time of day from it, but Joe enjoyed arm wrestling this one-armed bandit from time to time.

I called to him, and he appeared to be a bit startled. He turned, and I noticed he wasn't wearing his dentures. He told me his old set had cracked and he was waiting on the new ones. His face was drawn and it was accentuated more since the teeth were missing. I made eye contact and we talked. He had severe circulation problems in his feet and legs; mainly due to his diabetes. This was something I'd found to be a huge problem in the elderly, and Joe was one of the worst cases I'd seen.

We talked and he told me he'd come back down the following Sunday and be a part of the service.

That next Sunday arrived and so did Joe. He waited until everyone was seated and the service began. He sat behind most of the people in the second room. I knew he was embarrassed, and I didn't blame him.

In the past, he was always dressed in dress slacks, dress shoes, and oftentimes a shirt and tie since "That's the way you're supposed to go to church." On this day, he wore sweatpants, surgical wraps on his feet and a button up shirt.

This was one of those Sunday services that I asked the congregation to repeat the "Sinner's Prayer" with me. I watched as Joe repeated each and every word.

When the prayer was over, I asked the question, "If that was the first time you'd ever said that prayer and you meant it, raise your hand."

Joe's hand rose at the same time as his head. His eyes were filled with tears, and he quickly turned his scooter around and left for his room.

He returned to church the following Sunday. He was sporting a complete suit (although he was not wearing socks and his shoes were untied due to the swelling of his feet.) His new "smile" adorned him, and he looked like he was as sparkly as a game show host! He looked good, felt as good as he possibly could and couldn't wait until the end of the service.

His scooter was parked as close to the front as he could get and he never hesitated for a moment to ask for the microphone as the second syllable of "Amen" left my lips from the closing prayer.

I leaned over and reminded him that we were only doing Christian songs or hymns, and he let me know under no uncertain circumstances was this anything more than a song that will "lift people's spirits and fill their hearts."

Amazed at his response, but still a bit reluctant, I handed Joe the microphone. Everyone sat in perfect silence as Joe sang. I can't recall the song, but it was either a Sinatra tune or perhaps Tony Bennett's rendition of "The Way You Look Tonight."

I had been conned and by one of the best. As he began the song many of the residents recognized it from his recent karaoke performance and just shook their heads. Others made their exodus from the room. Joe was not the least bit phased. He was holding a microphone and could hear himself singing over a sound system. He was content. He was happy. He was performing!

We lost Joe that same year; he was eighty-five years old when he died. I was asked to do the memorial service for him. When I began speaking of this "Eighty some-year-old" man—I let everyone know that I felt like I was more of an emcee for him rather than the minister who was there to celebrate his life.

If Joe was there—he'd be singing, and for a brief moment, I think we all could hear his voice—repeating those last words—for the third and final time.

Chapter 4: What Does It Look Like?

Church Service Format

Our format is a simple one:
    1. call the service to order
    2. sing 2 hymns

3. pray

4.collect the offering (3rd song is sung during offering)

5. deliver the message (10-15 minutes)

6. share communion

7. close with a prayer.

Your mileage may vary, but whatever you do—stay consistent with the format you establish. Some people don't like change, and since this is a big change in their lives, they like to be able to follow along without further change.

Music

The music that is performed during the service is special. It is important to remember who your congregation is. Hymns that they heard as small children are what attract these people. They spark an old memory from their early years . . . one that was safe and comfortable and loving. Such songs as "Amazing Grace," "Rock of Ages," and "In the Garden" are staples with this age group.

We provide each member with lyric sheets for that day. At one time we thought it best to simply print out every lyric sheet we had and assemble them into small booklets. The cost could be recovered easily, but having watched some of our elderly members with some of the afflictions that accompany their senior years, we thought it best to keep things simple. Arthritis, failing eyesight and being discouraged with short term memory issues all needed to take a back seat to the mission at hand. So the old fashioned "keep it simple" method works best for us.

We simply take the lyric sheets for the songs selected and staple them together. These sheets are given out as each person is welcomed into the room. They are gathered at the same time the offering is collected, and it causes very little (if any) disruption to the flow of the service.

I have a slight tendency to add a little humor by saying, "if you will please open your hymn books to page one," and smiles erupt. When you're able to look out at your congregation and see all those smiles, believe me when I say, you have just received a blessing you'll never forget!

The sheets can be unstapled and reused time and again. We are still using some of the copies that we've had since the very beginning of our ministry. We're not super careful with them, but the shelf life is actually quite good.

I've found over the years that keeping the ceremony to no longer than 30–40 minutes is essential. Attention spans seem to waiver after that— not to mention their aged bodies have a tendency to develop cramps and muscle strains. Thirty minutes has always seemed to be the optimum length.

At the end of the service, we grab our guitars and usually add an extra song or two— depending on the liveliness of the crowd.

NOTE: For those who do not have someone available to lead worship or play a musical instrument, we have available a music CD or online downloads that include the hymns previously mentioned and many others. A simple CD player is all that is required. Lyric sheets are also available. See our website (www.320ministries.org) *for details.*

Sheriff Joe

Joe is his name.

He's ninety-one years old. He's barely five foot five inches tall and is as tough as they come. Joe has a thick Yankee accent, rugged Italian complexion and loves each and every person who passes in his path.

He must carry at least 100 lollipops with him at any given time. Rarely is there a man, woman or child who hasn't received one from him. His heart is huge! For some reason, Joe wears a five point gold star with the word "Sheriff" on it. It's a novelty badge, but we still call him "Sheriff Joe." He smiles.

When we first began our ministry in the lower main community room, we had to rearrange the furniture. There are four tables about 32 inches in diameter in the room; each with three to four chairs surrounding them. This room opens to the patio at the back of the building, which is where the tables are moved when we perform our service.

One Sunday, we came in and found all the tables already on the patio and the chairs neatly aligned into two perfect rows. No one took credit for the transformation, so we accepted it as a gift and continued with our set up of the sound equipment, speakers, etc. This continued for about three weeks until we found out that our own "Sheriff Joe" had been doing this for us. I called him out on it and all he did was smile.

We came in one Sunday and Joe was in a wheelchair. He had something wrong with his legs, and I stopped before entering the room to see if we could do anything for him. He indicated that he was okay . . . just a little problem.

"Oh yeah—the room is set up for ya!"

He still managed to drag four tables out the door and set up the chairs; and doing it in a wheelchair! Joe rarely sits in the same room as the rest of the congregation. He sits in the corridor listening intently to the music and the message. He partakes of communion and is a vital member of our ministry.

CHAPTER 5: TOPICS FOR SERMONS

I cannot begin to impress upon you the importance of this section. Over these past few years I've caught myself studying my seniors. I've found them to be attentive for the most part AS LONG AS THE MESSAGE IS PERTINENT TO THEIR LIVES.

I've used videos since there is a large flat screen television and DVD player at our disposal; I've done my best to improvise to keep things interesting, and even worn bib overalls to let them know I'm "ready for the harvest."

There are some things that will distract from your message, so be prepared for it and don't allow it to bother you. We are in a common area that has a popcorn machine, coffee pot, and ice cream bar in it. I've had people walk in front of my podium during a sermon and through a room full of people to get a cup of coffee numerous times. I smile and invite them to stay.

Many of the folks that attend our service can't wait to hear from family and to hear a cell phone ring during communion is nothing new. They actually answer it and begin a conversation as well.

I've had many people drop things, push their "attendant's button" which hangs around their necks because they wanted a glass of water or needed to leave to use the restroom. Some are either on new medications or just plain tired and will fall asleep. Some have even snored so loud that I had to make a joke about my lesson plan for the day. Don't be discouraged! You will receive a much larger blessing just being in their presence than you will ever give.

I've always made it a point to bring in other guests to speak. I would never want the service to be about my wife or myself (although we have gotten very attached to so many there). We've also been blessed to have a half dozen or so committed volunteers to help us (and you will need them!).

When you do have others bring a message to these people, you must remind them of who their audience is. They are people who deserve your respect; people who have fought for their country, lived full lives, helped build this great nation and who are intelligent people. I learned this the hard way when one young man brought a message that included the ills of pornography. Some of our congregation of seniors up into their nineties don't even know how to turn on a computer!

Messages need relevancy to these people. His message would have been great for high school to college age kids, but not here.

There are four main topics that I have found that have weighed heavy on the minds of the residents. They are: Death, Money, Loss of a Partner and Loneliness.

I want to briefly touch on each one of these, as they may not be as they appear. I have managed to talk to many of the residents about each one and their responses in many cases surprised me.

Death

Surprisingly enough, many of the people I've spoken with are not afraid of dying. In many cases, they are ready for it. These people have "worn out old bodies that don't work like they used to," as one person told me. "Waking up without pain would be a blessing—not waking up would be even better."

The first time I heard someone tell me that, I was pretty much shocked. My immediate response was "Don't talk like that!" But having heard it many times over these past few years, my current response is "Wouldn't that be great! Having a new body perfect in every way and being able to spend eternity with Jesus would be INCREDIBLE!" Letting each person know there is something to look forward to—as was promised: "I go to prepare a place for you"(John 14:2 KJV)—brings comfort. There is almost an immediate peace and a euphoric state of dreaming that seems to enter the conversation.

I hear about daily routines that begin with a regiment of taking upwards of fifteen pills to begin the morning. Getting dressed (or being assisted with getting dressed) to join everyone in the dining room for the morning meal can be a task that oftentimes some people will pass up. Some of the ladies just don't want to be seen without their hair fixed and their faces painted. Vanity failed to escape some as the years passed by.

For others, it's a time when they feel their worst. Joints and muscles ache and the process of "waking up" is very stressful for many. One thing I've found with the topic of death is to be honest. These people can smell a lie a mile away, so be kind—and be honest. No one has ever left this earth without dying. People are good with that. Most of them are concerned about "how" they will die.

Allow them to express their fears, but always give the reassurance that regardless of how it happens, there will always be the love of others to help them through it.

In the 6 years I have pastored our ministry—I have performed numerous memorials or funerals. I recall after my third one, I went to my pastor and told him I didn't think I could continue this ministry if for no other reason—this part of it.

He smiled and told me it was just something that "came with the territory." I'll never forget his words:

"You have to have the heart of a lamb and the hide of a rhino."

I'll be the first to admit that it's a difficult combination. We've grown close to so many of the residents that I feel like I've buried my own parents and grandparents many times over. Then I sit back, and listen to the very words I've spoken to them; the part where Jesus is waiting for us to come home and how He has promised us eternal life. I've learned to cry again, and I'm not ashamed to tell you. Don't be afraid to cry with someone, but just remind them:

"Don't cry because it's over—smile because it happened." —Dr. Seuss

If you can get someone to talk about themselves, ask them what they would like most to be remembered for in their lives. Choose your words carefully—not to frighten but to learn. You will be amazed and surprised at the responses you'll receive. They've helped me with many a memorial service.

Money

Many people are afraid they won't have enough money to live out the rest of their lives, and this is a very real concern of the elderly. Investments over the years have gone bad along with the economy—much of which were never updated when they were first made years ago.

I become easily angered when I discover that many seniors have "fallen victim" to scams and crimes against the elderly, but even more so when I find they have had family members do much the same. I have never offered to take, hold or manage anyone's finances, nor do I recommend any such actions—even when asked. There are many agencies that help in preparing and maintaining financial situations, and I simply have the people request it through the staff and counselors provided within the home. There are also many government agencies that will help supervise and oversee any misuse as well. When it comes to comforting someone whose main concerns are food and shelter, I simply remind them to "Cast all your anxiety on Him because He cares for you."(1 Peter 5:7 NIV) If God can provide for the smallest of the birds—how much more do you think He cares about His children?

This may need to become a reminder until such time when they are more comfortable with the subject. Seeing that they had breakfast, lunch and dinner and that they had their own bed to sleep in are just a few of the ways to provide reassurance.

Loss of a Partner

I will tell you right now, there is nothing—absolutely NOTHING you can say or do that will remove the feeling of emptiness due to the loss of a partner. It will bring tears to your eyes and an aching in your heart even if you never met the spouse who died.

To the surviving husband or wife, it's one of the greatest tragedies they would ever experience less the death of a child. The spouse who died was chosen to be with them for life. I've performed funeral services for those who were married for over sixty years. The shallow look of loss is unbelievable, and my eyes fill with tears as I sit here and write about this even now.

The depression is so great that oftentimes, the surviving partner follows soon after. Providing support and allowing the partner to grieve is vital, and it is an important process. I don't tell anyone not to cry, but I encourage it; the same as I do when I tell them to laugh at the funny and good times together.

We're all human and we hurt when we lose someone close to us. We also hurt when we see someone we care about who is in pain. After all, Jesus wept when Lazarus died—who are we not to?

One thing I have found that helps more than anything—is to be able to ask questions and listen. Allowing someone to grieve means more than just holding their hand while they cry. There is a part of us that wants to brag about our partners. Accomplishments, attitudes, trips they've shared, vacations, school, graduations, their children, careers; they all become a huge part of their lives' stories, and be prepared to share in them. If you weren't important in their lives, you wouldn't be invited to listen so take this as a major compliment and share in their enjoyment or sorrow.

Reminding them that one day they'll be reunited in heaven gives them the hope of something to look forward to.

I spoke with one gentleman whose wife had passed away after seventy years of marriage. I was concerned about his attitude toward life and just came right out and asked him "Now that she's gone, how do you feel about life?"

His answer astounded me. "I miss her something awful bad—but I'm in no hurry to see her any time soon!" We both had a great laugh and that was that.

Loneliness

Believe it or not, loneliness is one of the most difficult things to not only discuss, but to help find a solution.

It's hard to believe that anyone could be lonely when they live in a building with over one hundred fifty other people. They share the same line when they await their medication, see one another during activities and eat together in the dining room. Many of them return to their rooms alone, and as one 92 year old lady told me, "I just went back to my room to cry." Some of this is either due to the loss of a spouse or the feeling of being rejected by family. "They just stuck me here so I wouldn't be a burden."

In many cases, it's a matter of educating them to the amount of care they need. Most family homes are not equipped with wheelchair ramps, much less the openness required for wheelchair access. Looking at our own home, we would need to get rid of half our furniture and remodel bathrooms to accommodate someone who required this kind of care; not to mention the skill and training.

Once the resident realizes, acknowledges, and accepts the fact that it took a lot of love to help make this life changing decision, their lives become more at ease. I've had people who came to me the following Sunday that they missed service and apologized saying "My son came by with his family and took me out to breakfast; I'm so sorry that I missed service." I just laugh, share a hug and say "Anytime you get to be with your family, take it."

There are many cases where the resident is alone; very alone. In some instances due to finances, insurance or other circumstances, a wife or husband requires care that the partner cannot provide and they must live in an assisted living facility away from their spouse. Oftentimes, the place of residence is in another state. In other cases, there is no surviving spouse or family, and the person is left to fend for themselves. This is not uncommon, but in most cases, a child or some other relative is there to assist in not only finding the "right" facility, but also reassures the family member that they will be there for them.

Many times you'll find that these words, although said with the greatest of intentions, cannot be adhered to due to the busyness of their own lives and those of their family. Missing just one day of visiting can become emotionally devastating to a resident. This is where a strong ministry makes a difference; one that helps to insure the "family of God" has a strong presence within the assisted living community. I encourage each and every member of our congregation to "check-in" on one another. "Look around and see the empty chairs. You know who normally sits there, so stop by and let them know you missed them this morning. If they're not feeling well, ask if you can pray with them. They'll do the same for you one day as well."

When new residents arrive they are usually timid, in need of some orientation, and especially friendship. Each person there can relate to one (if not all) of the issues they are facing when they first moved into the home. Loneliness at this time is at an all-time high. Even fear can be a constant burden as well. Make a friend and be a friend.

Making sure that no one was "sent there to die" but to LIVE is essential. Where we serve, it's now a part of the orientation phase to mention that there is a Catholic and Christian/Protestant service available each and every Sunday morning.

Don't be surprised if they come searching you out to become a part of your ministry.

Cleaveland

This gentleman is just that; a gentleman in every sense of the word.
I've been to his apartment and everything is kept neat and tidy. His wife also lives at the same location; however she is in a separate part of the building. She has Alzheimer's disease and has all but lost all her memory of everything. That includes their 29 year marriage and the memories they built and shared together over those years.

Six days out of the week, he walks over to the Memory Care unit, and takes his lovely wife by the hand and brings her back to his apartment. He was married previously, and his first wife had passed away many years prior. He was taking "extra special care" of this woman regardless of how their lives had arrived at the place where they are today.

His current wife has no recollection of things between. She just knows that this handsome gent comes every day and takes her by the hand and sits with her.

His next few moments of conversation with me left me astounded. He told me that he turns on some music and she scoffs at him saying "I wish you'd turn that off—that's the music you listened to your old wife with." Knowing that she's not the same woman he married and that the disease has taken over, he simply turns off the music.

He turns on the television and her comments lead to the near same response. He turns off the TV and simply asks "What would you like to do?"

Her response is simple . . . "I'm fine just sitting here with you and holding your hand."

So for the past year, six days a week, he goes there. He escorts her back to his apartment where they sit side by side, and hold hands. The four hour visit ends and he walks her back to her room.

Today I've learned more about love, compassion, and patience than I ever have. He told me that he knows she won't even remember the visit 15 minutes after he takes her back to her room, but for those precious few hours a day . . . she's there with the man who loves her.

CHAPTER 6: FUNDING

A Quick Look at What It "Doesn't" Cost

This topic has raised its head time after time. I've had many church leaders tell me, "We just don't have it in the budget."

My reply is "You can't afford not to have it in your budget."

Let's get down to dollars and cents. In the beginning, ours didn't cost a dime. My wife and I had guitars and an amplifier, which at the time was extreme overkill. As the ministry grew, so did our needs. I was preaching through a guitar amp and a microphone.

As the size of the room(s) began to increase, so did the need for my voice to project. My wife has a beautiful voice, but it is not loud. We personally invested in a sound system to the tune of around $300. I had a definite advantage because I used to have a band that performed around Las Vegas, so some of the equipment had already been obtained. For others, $300 may as well be $3,000.

There is no reason why a beginning ministry can't be done without the need for amplification. In some instances, the facility may already have a sound system or even possibly a karaoke machine that could be used. God will provide what is necessary—He did for us. As of today, we have a 200 watt sound system, two speakers on stands, microphone and music stands, a 16 channel mixer, cables, monitors, several microphones, and amplifier. If we have guest musicians stop by with their keyboards, guitars, violins, etc., we can accommodate them with sound.

We also celebrate each service with the Lord's Supper. We purchase the juice cups and wafers from the local Christian book store. These are minimal cost items as is the grape juice. A simple glass bowl with plastic lid can be obtained for a few dollars at any discount store and can double as a storage container for the unused wafers.

In the early days of our ministry, we did not take up an offering. After just a few months, the residents asked if they could help support the ministry by getting the opportunity to give financially. We then began taking up a weekly offering. We have it "earmarked" for this ministry and substantial amounts of donations were given. These funds can be used to purchase the needed supplies and still enable us to have money left over to assist other ministries within the church.

Although we still personally own the sound system, more than enough money has been given in just a few short months to purchase one.

Understand that the largest expenditure you will have for this ministry—is someone's time. It will take someone with determination, drive, commitment and an undying love for people.

My wife Lori and I are a team. We went into this ministry in much prayer and we look forward to one day passing the torch to others to continue what was started, to get others to see the need for such a vital ministry and begin one themselves.

We pray it becomes a desire for you as well.

Gracie

Gracie. I'm not really certain how many years over 100 she was, nor do I believe she knew either.

Gracie was a little lady. It takes a while to "gauge" how tall someone is when they are confined to a wheelchair. Petiteness is apparent when the feet touch the floor boards that are adjusted very high on the chair.

Gracie appeared to be fragile, but wanted to hug and have as much contact with anyone within reach. Even at her age of being a "centurion," she never dozed off or fell asleep in our church services. She would listen intently; as if she was studying for "final exams."

There were times when I sat in the room as someone else would preach for me, and Gracie would have a bit of a distant look in her eyes. I often thought that my sitting beside her confused her since I wasn't at the pulpit. I've noticed over these past five years in this ministry, that many people at that age tend to begin to lose their short-term memory. I'm beginning to believe that the "early years" were the most memorable, and we all often revert back to the happier times in our lives.

One thing about Gracie, she never forgot the words to any of the old hymns or gospel songs, and even at her age, she had the voice of a beautiful songbird. I had never noticed that in the past since I was a full room's distance from her. Sitting beside her, I could hear the most angelic voice I could ever hear coming from a tiny lady.

I reached over and patted her on the hand during one of the songs. Midway through the message, she reached over and placed her hand on mine; oftentimes patting it, but mostly just resting on it.

She is now with Jesus, and I know He is listening to that beautiful voice singing the praises of her Heavenly Father.

Chapter 7: Final Thoughts

One of the greatest blessings we have received since the inception of the ministry is being able to witness people who have accepted Jesus Christ as their Lord and Savior. As I stated earlier, one would think that at this stage in their lives people's minds would have been set on their faith and beliefs. But we have found that not to be the case.

What a blessing it is to see God's love unfold in this way. It's been a blessing that God has allowed my wife and me to be a part of, and it's our prayer that others will do the same.

There are no set rules on what works and what doesn't. The Holy Spirit will guide you along if you will only ask. What you've been reading here is what we have found to be spiritually sound and graciously received with our congregation.

The easiest thing to do is to ask. Don't waiver from the Word—be sure that whoever takes this ministry has a love for the elderly. A couple equally yoked with the love of the elderly is a good start.

Honesty served up with a helping of love will take you a long way. These folks have a lot of wisdom they can impart and are willing to share. They can also smell out a lie, so be honest. My first time to preach came six years ago at this ministry. I let them know it when I first stepped up and all I could do was pray for wisdom and mercy. I've never looked back since that first day—nor will I ever forget it.

Thank you for taking the time to read and study what we've been sharing with you in this program. Our prayer is that you will see the need and spread the Gospel of Jesus Christ to all people. "Religion that God our Father accepts as pure and faultless is this: to look after orphans and widows in their distress and to keep oneself from being polluted by the world. (James 1:27 NIV)

I encourage our congregation to do this as well among themselves. "What if we're not a widow?" one man boldly spoke up. I simply smiled and said that an orphan is one who has no parents—they have already gone to heaven. "With the average age in this room to be somewhere in the area of 87, I feel it's safe to say you're all orphans . . . so spread it around like that!" They laugh and move on.

God bless you in all you do in Jesus' great name. You will be rewarded as He has promised.

Jimmy's Story

I'll keep this short and sweet because none of this is about me. It never has been and never will be—it's about the love that Jesus has for all of us.

I was raised a Catholic—attended parochial schools all my life, and I feared God more than loved Him. I was taught about His wrath, what He would do if I committed a sin, and how I would burn in hell if I died with a sin on my soul.

I cannot recall ever being told about His love and how it was out of that love that He sent Jesus to die on the cross for me.

In my early twenties, I "got saved." I did what was asked of me and then got "wet" the following Sunday. Everyone thought I had been baptized, but nothing was ever explained to me. I repeated this again four years later. This time, I knew I had Christ in my life and in my heart. But for the next couple of decades, I lived for myself.

In my late fifties, I met a woman who lived for God. She sang His praises like an angel, and wanting her in my life more than I wanted anything else, I turned back to the

Savior I once turned my back on . . . and pretty much said "Let's do this!"

I had a successful career in the mechanical contracting field as a Senior Project Manager, and the six figure income was nice. I also had a country band performing up and down the famed Las Vegas Strip. All this would come to an end when I was asked to take up a ministry for the elderly at an assisted living facility and asked to preach. At the first request from my pastor, I was flippant and borderline arrogant.

I was asked to pray about it, which my wife and I did. The following Sunday a guy, who "got paid to get people to drink" in showrooms and casinos in Las Vegas, preached his first sermon. I've never looked back except to thank God for using me.

My wife and I have led this ministry since the fall of 2008. We have been extremely blessed by it. I tell you these things with no pride in my heart for what's been accomplished. I say these things—because God took a guy in his late fifties, changed his heart, and with no formal teaching used him for His honor and glory. If He can use me, he can use anyone. He will find someone for your ministry as well.

It is our prayer that you will not only accept the challenge of beginning a ministry for the elderly, but share this information with others.

May God bless you and what you are about to take upon yourselves and your church. The rewards are great—the blessings will flow in both directions.

—Pastor James E. McNamara

"God doesn't call the qualified; He qualifies the called."

About the Authors

Jimmy and Lori found each other late in life. Their first meeting was at an open mic night that Jimmy was hosting on the dock of a beautiful lakeside restaurant. It wasn't love at first sight, in fact, quite the opposite, but those feelings would soon change. God had other plans for this couple and on March 20th of 2008 the two, very much in love, became one in holy matrimony.

From the moment they were married it was obvious that God brought them together for a purpose that not even they had envisioned. Answering a call to lead worship at an assisted living center turned into a much greater commitment than they had anticipated. Jimmy had been called to preach—a call that would ultimately change both of their lives forever.

Along with pastoring the senior home ministry, Jimmy also performed weddings in the wedding capital of the world—Las Vegas. He was named the #2 wedding officiant by *Wedding Wire* and wrote *Tales from the Wedding Altar*—a book sharing hilarious, behind the scenes moments from weddings at which he has officiated.

Lori has had various careers in the public sector, but finds her greatest joy in serving the elderly. She has recently recorded a music CD titled: *Hymns That Take Me Home*. She continues the senior home ministry that she and Jimmy once shared for over six years and also serves as president of 320 Ministries International, a ministry she started soon after Jimmy's death to carry on the mission that God had placed on both their hearts.

320 MINISTRIES INTERNATIONAL

320 Ministries International was founded by Jimmy and Lori McNamara. Its purpose and mission is to bring awareness to the Christian community of the need and importance of bringing church to the elderly, and to provide resources to those interested in beginning their own elderly ministry.

It is the hope and desire of 320 Ministries International to connect churches with senior homes across the nation.

For more information,
please check out this website:
www.320ministries.org

Also by Pastor James E. McNamara

Tales from the Wedding Altar

When Pastor McNamara solemnly stood before wedding couples, he heard some outrageous things the guests never hear; like the bride saying to the groom, "I just felt the baby kick," or the groom saying to the bride, "This tux is giving me a wedgie."

"I have been performing weddings in Las Vegas for several years. There are things that I hear; things that I notice because prior to the ceremony, I am pretty much a wallflower and everyone feels comfortable speaking around someone they can't see. There are petty things spoken between jealous women (and men!) There are secrets revealed by the father of the bride no one hears, and most importantly, standing in very close proximity to the wedding couple at the altar where the closest people are four feet away; the small whispers between the couple are priceless!" —From the author

ISBN 978-1-938985-23-2 • 5 x 7 paperback • 144 pgs • $10.95

Available from
Christopher Matthews Publishing
www.ChristopherMatthewsPub.com
or fine bookstores on and off the internet.

Lightning Source UK Ltd.
Milton Keynes UK
UKHW02f0632170118
316275UK00018B/494/P